America of We the People

Terry Overton

Copyright © 2021 Terry Overton

All rights reserved.

ISBN: 9798479312175

Bible verses from The Holy Bible, NIV, Copyright 1984

DEDICATION

For my dad, Kenneth F. Meier, who earned three purple hearts serving as a Marine in the Korean War, Fox Company, 2nd Battalion, 1st Marine Division (Fleet Marine Force).

For my grandson, Jackson Leonard, who serves protecting our country in the 82nd Airborne.

For all the brave men and women who were in Afghanistan, August 2021, Adam Ely and his brothers and sisters of the 82nd Airborne, 501:2 Geronimo, and members of other branches of service.

For Pack Sheffield, Captain 1st Logistical Command, Vietnam 1970.

For James Watson Overton, Jr. Seaman Second Class 1944-1946.

For all service divisions including Navy, Coast Guard, Army, Air Force, Marines.

For my son, Jake Adam Leonard, and all the brave firefighters and first responders who keep us safe at home no matter the hour.

For my husband, Frank Overton, and all the Overton family who serve or did serve in law enforcement, holding the Blue Line, here on the homeland.

For all State Troopers and Border Patrol who fight to keep our borders safe.

Thank you all for your service.

AMERICA OF WE THE PEOPLE

IN MEMORY

In memory of Kenneth E. Lewis and Jennifer Lewis who lost their lives on September 11, 2001, on flight 77.

In memory of all those who died on September 11, 2001, those perished in Benghazi September 11, 2012, the victims of the attack on the USS Cole October 12, 2000, those who lost their lives on August 26, 2021, in Afghanistan, and all other brave men and women who died due to terror attacks against the United States and who perished during combat, fighting for freedom.

In memory of Americans who perished from terrorists attacks August 7, 1998 Nairobi, Kenya, and Dar es Salaam, Tanzania; December 31, 2019, January 1, 2020, Bagdad, 1983 Beirut.

In memory of Floyd McClanie Myers, Company F, 309th Infantry Regiment, 78th Division of the U.S. Ninth Army who died on January 12, 1945, in Belgium, and for all who perished in WWI, WWII, Korean War, Vietnam, Gulf War, Dessert Storm, and Operation Enduring Freedom.

TERRY OVERTON

Table of Contents

DEDICATION iii
IN MEMORY v

Patriotism *1*

Patriotism Quotes 2

Patriotism Poems and Musings *3*

A WOUNDED EAGLE 4

WHAT IS HAPPENING? 7

PATRIOTISM 9

TO KATHARINE LEE BATES 11

America the Beautiful 11

MY WORN-OUT FRIEND 14

Soldiers and Wars *17*

Soldiers and Wars Quotes 18

Soldiers and Wars Poems and Musings *19*

A YOUNG SOLDIER OFF TO WAR 20

I DID NOT KNOW YOU THEN 21

HILL 749 23

JOHNSON'S 'NAM 24

END OF 'NAM 26

ON A PERFECT MORNING SHATTERED 28

11 September 2001 28

BILLOWING CLOUDS OF DESTRUCTION
.... 29

GOLD STARS IN HEAVEN 30

26 August 2021 30

SOLDIERS DID WHAT THEY 33

WERE SENT TO DO 33

31 August 2021 33

First Responders and the Homeland 35

First Responders and the Homeland 36

Quotes 36

First Responders and the Homeland Poems and Musings 37

FIREFIGHTERS' PASSION 38

REMEMBERING BLUE 40

BORDER GUARDS 41

WE SAW YOU THERE 42

Current State of Affairs 43

Current State of Affairs 44

Quotes 44

Current State of Affairs Poems and Musings .45

TRUTH 46

REPORTING AND WRITING OF
YESTERYEAR AND TODAY 47

BIG TECH RULES THE WORLD 49

JUST BECAUSE YOU SAY IT'S SO 50

OUR BORDER FROM BOTH SIDES...........52

IDENTITY OF WE THE PEOPLE...............55

INSIDE OUT 57

OUR SECOND AMENDMENT 59

'ISMS 60

PANDEMIC..62

GENDER IDENTITY 63

Leaders Around the World 65

Leaders Around the World...............................66

Quotes 66

Leaders Around the World Poems and Musings 67

WHERE ARE THE CHURCHILLS? 68

ONE LIFE CHANGES THE WORLD 70

PEACEFUL HERO: TANKMAN 71

PEACEFUL HERO: AUNG SAN SUU KYI...72

One Nation Under God..................................73

    One Nation Under God 74

    Quotes 74

One Nation Under God Poems and Musings **75**

    AMERICA, WE PRAY FOR YOU 76

    IN WHAT DIRECTION SHOULD 79

    WE GO? 79

    NATIONS AND GOD 81

    PRAY FOR OUR FUTURE 82

    AND WHAT OF OUR FUTURE?...................83

    WHAT ARE THE LESSONS LEARNED?....84

Where is Our Hope ? 87

    Where is Our Hope? 88

    Quotes 88

Where is Our Hope? Poems and Musings......89

    HOW WE BUILT AMERICA 90

    WE MUST DO THIS 92

    LAST WORD: GOD IS OUR STRENGTH 95

Patriotism

Patriotism Quotes

"Loyalty to country ALWAYS. Loyalty to government, when it deserves it." ---Mark Twain

"A government big enough to give you everything you want is a government big enough to take from you everything you have". ---Multiple Attributions.

"In the beginning of a change, the patriot is a scarce man, and brave, and hated, and scorned. When his cause succeeds, the timid join him, for then it costs nothing to be a patriot." ---Mark Twain.

"Patriotism means to stand by the country. It does not mean to stand by the president or any other public official, save exactly to the degree in which he himself stands by the country. It is patriotic to support him insofar as he efficiently serves the country. It is unpatriotic not to oppose him to the exact extent that by inefficiency or otherwise he fails in his duty to stand by the country. In either event, it is unpatriotic not to tell the truth, whether about the president or anyone else." ---Theodore Roosevelt

Patriotism Poems and Musings

TERRY OVERTON

A WOUNDED EAGLE

A wounded eagle lies on the ground
Its splendid feathers strewn around
Not from afar a bullet flew
But from within, before she knew

And next to her Old Glory slumped
By disrespecting people, dumped
Fiercely carried into battle times
Now stomping her is not a crime

A preacher cries to just a few
"Before us lies red, white, and blue"
Men died protecting her and us
Now no one wants to make a fuss

And from His mighty face we see
A tear rolls down for you and me
"How can these people stand idly by
And watch their sacred freedom die?

"This great nation founded under Me
Now says 'don't stand, take a knee'
Don't people know from times of old
To bravely pray and to be bold?"

For only with God's power and cover
Will this mighty land recover

AMERICA OF WE THE PEOPLE

A Wounded Eagle, cont.

Believers hang their heads and cry
Our nation burns, and cities die

Our leaders know not where they go
Down foreign paths our monies flow
And now, with evil motivation
There is a plan to ruin this nation

"We're all the same as everyone
Our nation shouldn't outshine a one
We will spread our funds around
And invite trespassers on our grounds"

Our Father once again is weeping
And wonders "Why are my people sleeping?
If they change their evil ways and come to me
This nation will be strong, and free"

Crickets are the only sound
Heard across this hallowed ground
And in their graves the soldiers cry
"Please help them Lord, our freedom dies"
Fall on your knees this day and pray
Dear Father don't let us end this way
Please tell us now what to do
To return to freedom and honor You

Comes from on high His mighty roar
"I can help you out no more
It is up to you to gather people
Save My country, temples, steeples

A Wounded Eagle, cont.

"For My nation is in great upheaval
Sinking under depths of evil
Only one thing remains for you to do
Join together; pray for red, white, and blue

"Through faith alone you will be saved
Too few have My faith displayed
I will weep to watch you fail
But greet you in heaven as others find hell

"Be strong, be kind, love each other always
No matter what happens, you'll have finer days
For in Me your faith you place
And you will see My shining face."

WHAT IS HAPPENING?

We are in a strange place in time and history; at times it feels surreal. You might wonder if we are in a different place, no longer our United States. The current administration grasps for more power and control. The administration is overstepping authority while increasing their own power and domination over the citizenry. Mandates for our own personal health? Abandonment of American citizens? Not living up to our promises with international communities? No borders of our country? Can this be happening in our world? Is this our country?

We continue, we worry. We do not know the ending or where we will go. We are on the road to somewhere that only God knows.

We are called to play our part in this journey. We can no longer remain silent. To be heard, we must speak.

With God at our side, and us on His side, we will be where He places us, each one for His purpose.

Never forget the first three words of the United States Constitution: We the People.

What's Happening? cont.

The end is planned. Hold on to Him and each other. The end of our journey will be magnificent no matter what happens.

He has written our future.

PATRIOTISM

Our world seems upside down. Patriotism is suddenly a controversial term. Some say patriotism is not something to be admired. If you speak of it, you may be heckled or attacked. Honest love of country is not allowed-it is evil now to express your feelings as a patriot.

That is not what I say.

Patriotism means you feel your country in the extreme depths of your heart, the innermost part of your pride. Patriotism is loyalty, fidelity, allegiance, and single-mindedness of your conviction to your country.

For many brave men and women, it means giving up their own personal lives so ordinary citizens can remain in the comfort of their own homes, read a book, plant a garden, write, go to work, or church, or to social gatherings freely in our great America. While we can travel state-to-state on family

Patriotism, cont.

vacations, soldiers are sent on missions, all over the world, sleeping and surviving in foreign countries, fighting for our freedom, and protecting others under tyrant's rule.

Patriotism conceptually is considerably larger than a single person and yet each person plays a vital role in keeping patriotism alive. In the United States, patriotism means being part of a country centered on freedom and founded on faith. We value respect and love for others.

People in other countries only dream about patriotism.

Pray to strengthen our country, to invoke a mighty power of God and infuse patriotism across the country, and to unite with others to keep fighting for our freedom.

TO KATHARINE LEE BATES
America the Beautiful

I wonder if those who criticize the view of America seen by your eyes, understand the admiration you had when you climbed majestic purple mountains? Have they ever seen the magnificence of amber fields of grain?

Do they know the year was 1893 when you penned the words they call outdated and absurd?

Do they think these cherished words are no longer true?

Do they not understand brotherhood is included as part of the very fabric of our nation?

Why do they think the grace of God is not present from sea to shining sea?

America the Beautiful, cont.

Are they looking across the miracle we call United States?

They don't comprehend; it's too complex to see,
staring at their phones or TV.

Look up, look back, in history,
before you tear it down.

Are they depending on media sound bites for their knowledge of America?

To those who say the words of *America the Beautiful* are irrelevant: open your mind and study what's been found to be the most unique country in all the world. Examine other countries and you will know it was God's grace that made it so.

America the Beautiful, cont.

Our land is a land grander than any other.

Look outside yourself, look at your patriotic sisters and brothers.

Ask yourself, why do others from foreign lands want to live here?

It is unresponsible for anyone to live in this great country of the United States of America and not understand our country's history and values. Do not complain without knowledge.

You are blessed to be in the United States of America. You are blessed to live in America the Beautiful. Embrace it.

MY WORN-OUT FRIEND

The pink tint of day's tired end
Made you appear sad, my friend
You barely waved as I passed by
Your stripes drooped low, as if to cry

Before you were fully grown
Your country split in two and groaned
And mended back together again
You grew more stars and stripes my friend

Through other wars you stood tall
The United States did not fall
The Constitution spelled it out
Our freedom round the world stood out

But now you hang your stripes so low
You fear that freedom soon will go
And our unique experiment
Will be captured by socialists' intent

If you are reading this verse today
Don't let your freedom slip away
Years past in its history
Our flag enjoyed proud victories

My Worn-Out Friend, cont.

Gazing at white stars on blue
A wakeup call is overdue
The country populous now asleep
I now know my friend why you weep

TERRY OVERTON

Soldiers and Wars

Soldiers and Wars Quotes

"It is fatal to enter a war without the will to win it." ---Douglas MacArthur

"To be prepared for war is one of the most effective means of preserving peace." ---George Washington

"Age wrinkles the body, quitting wrinkles the soul." --- Douglas MacArthur

"No good decision was ever made in a swivel chair." ---George S. Patton

"Pessimism never won any battle." ---Dwight D. Eisenhower

Soldiers and Wars Poems and Musings

TERRY OVERTON

A YOUNG SOLDIER OFF TO WAR

We sent you off to war not knowing
You returned, your eyes not glowing
Stark changes on your face now showing
You'd met hate eye to eye

Your boundless energy and infinite smile
Relentless future of unending miles
Now waned; you had seen the reaper close
"Death to America!" the demons boast

Your jaw now tight with eyes so worn
The depth of innocence had been torn
And in your soul and heart we see
Your fear of death not yet set free

When you returned to your homeplace
Life went on, undisturbed in pace
The people here did not relate
To distant fear, death, and hate

Our soldier now returned from war
Sees the truth of the devil's score
The demon lives in hearts of hate
Unknowing people can't relate
To the pain and sorrow felt
The returned soldier prayed and knelt
He asked for peace to blanket earth
Now he's aware of war's worth

I DID NOT KNOW YOU THEN

I did not know you then.
I had not met you yet
To the 38th parallel you went
To keep South Korea free
Demanding Chinese soldiers flee
You went away to bravely fight
With bullets piercing in dead of night

I did not know you when
The frigid, cutting, bitter wind
Took frozen toes from feet of friends
Who fought bravely for communism's end

I did not know of your pain
When three purple hearts you sustained
To this day you have no regrets
Defending others from hate's threats

Years later into our lives you came
Just as a father, you were the same
Raised my mother's children,
Of different names
And instilled in us the love we know
To defend our country from its foes

And of the battles you seldom speak
Of brothers in arms, their stories unique
To teach us freedom's cost and blessings

I Did Not Know You Then, cont.

Now once again, we feel the pressing
Of evil destruction of our nation
And of threats of our annihilation

I pray for others as brave as you
Save us today from evils new

HILL 749

No one at home knew the stark terrain
The steep cliff and rough remains
Of a country torn by war
But 1st Marines were given the chore

Secure the hill, make progress forward
The Marines continued pushing onward
Squeaking sounds of machine guns' wheels
Announced the intruding movement of
The enemy who soon would pounce
Upon our Marine forces so brave
As countless soldiers found their grave

Fox Company fought through cold and rain
The morning found only twelve remained
Who survived the brutal fight
To secure Hill 749 that night

It's sad to know how many died
But you battled on and tried
To come back home where you had
A new life and became our dad.

I'm sorry for losses sustained
And know your life forever changed
But we are thankful for your years
Of raising us through smiles and tears.

TERRY OVERTON

JOHNSON'S 'NAM

Countless losses flashed before our eyes
The evening news always surprised
Those of us around TVs gathered
Watched the chaos, our world shattered
To see the names of so many killed
Around the world in jungle fields
Our older brothers and their friends
Horrifically changed, if returned at all
Due to politicians' actions
Vietnam refused to fall

Streets full of angry crowds rustling
Young people, unaware of suffering
Of heroes in war who did not recover
From the darkest evils known to man
When they returned to the homeland
We owed them a lifetime of support
They remain neglected, from all reports

And those blessed to ride the freedom bird
Eyes glazed, empty of tears, shell-shocked from months before
Found no parade or cheers waiting at their door
Only jeers, wives long departed; what could they do?
After giving years and lives for you

No tickertape on main street proceeded
Not even a simple "Thank you," greeted

Johnson's 'Nam, cont.

Our men whose lives forever changed
Arriving home, protests remained.

Over one million military and civilian lives were lost
And those forever disabled? another cost

Poor decisions,
Carried out bravely
By those under the Commander-in-Chief
Heroes of Johnson's 'Nam

END OF 'NAM

There are some things not meant to see
The blood of war, the agony
Of people fighting hand-to-hand
Of bodies littered across a land

Our soldiers witnessed morbid sights
Of bombs morphing dark to light
Extinguishing lives through the night
Exploding noises, shrieking bullets, fright
When morning broke the land had changed
Scarcely few living souls remained

On the news, we watched and cried
As limping, wheeling, they arrived
And home from war they'd sadly come
They knew they'd left victory undone
Tormenting cries of embroiled souls
Who fought to defend freedom,
As they were told

Back home in pieces they soon came
Never more to be the same
Some shells of souls remained among
The others injured bodies young
How can we repay the price
They paid for us, when sent to fight?

End of 'Nam, cont.

Black granite walls contain the names
More than fifty thousand the reaper gained
Too early were their lives claimed
Mourning families buried remains
The end of 'Nam

TERRY OVERTON

ON A PERFECT MORNING SHATTERED
11 September 2001

The sun was bright, sky vibrant, clear
No one knew of danger near

A phone call pierced through the perfect calm
"Two planes crashed buildings. Were there bombs?"

The towers fell, other planes were downed
Terrorists invaded our sacred ground

A haunting thought overwhelmed my brain
America, our nation, won't be the same

No longer trusting all we see
Temporarily brought down to our knees

That morning we won't soon forget
Our nation will be stronger yet

BILLOWING CLOUDS OF DESTRUCTION

First impressions were unbelievable
How could a plane fly into the tower?
But then another one followed
And the message was clear
Terrorism was here

The clouds of debris thick and fast
Blanketed the ground, streets, people
Now covered with ash

The screams, the shouts, the cries of people hurting
The running, panic, sorrowful wondering of those not returned
Who went to work as any day,
Now it's twenty years they've been away

And sadly, twenty years to the day
The terrorists cheer in their streets
My heart breaks

TERRY OVERTON

GOLD STARS IN HEAVEN
26 August 2021

You see up in the heavens tonight
New souls who bravely fought our fight
Hoisted up by angels' wings
Now songs of sorrow we all sing

Our brave ones lifted high this night
They fought for *us*; it was *our* fight
Against an evil lurking round
Where now is goodness to be found?

The ever-present danger lingers
While politicians point their fingers
It was not the soldiers' plan
But those in office in our land

Father we pray for wisdom now
As those in charge who took a vow
Must plan to go and fight this fight
To uphold freedom and our rights

Evil grows much stronger now
Don't take your hand up from the plow
Abandonment of people will not work
The evil powers still will lurk
They wait for the moment right
To boldly strike in dead of night

AMERICA OF WE THE PEOPLE

Gold Stars in Heaven, cont.

Hit your knees, all who pray
Deliver us from evil's way

Restore this land to days of old
When parents did not have stars of gold

Our hearts are breaking for your tears
Please understand our hearts are near
We would not wish upon you pain
We pray for healing when Stars are lain
Beneath the ground to rest in peace
And now we pray that sorrows cease

Please Lord from hate our land deliver
Our prayers we ask you to consider
Provide us leadership of wisdom
From those who know of Your Kingdom

If into battle we must go
Provide a plan to make it so
Our fight will be swift and sure
Our land again must be secure
Free from evil's intrusive threat
And let no soldier feel regret

Gold Stars in Heaven, cont.

Leadership, do what is sound
Listen to boots upon the ground
Provide for us patriotic strength
Not unwon wars of years in length

Tonight, in peace the soldiers shine
These Stars of Gold now are Thine
They twinkle gold and light our night
Shining down from heavens bright

And pray if more Gold Stars join these in heaven
They will be for Your purpose given
Goodness will grow round the world
And respect felt when our flag unfurled

SOLDIERS DID WHAT THEY WERE SENT TO DO
31 August 2021

Soldiers did what they were sent to do
They rushed, were hushed, then followed through
Proud politicians boldly shout
"By 31 August, we got them out!"

The puppet on stage loudly laughs
"Before 9-11!" Then he gaffs
At his watch he looks and sighs
As thirteen flagged coffins glide sadly by

We mean no disrespect, the people cry
But how much longer for this guy?
As number two and three stand idly by
"Those two no better" the people cry.

A world away a country weakened
We are no longer their hopeful beacon
Now evil emboldened knocks on doors
"Give us your women, children, girls!"
Our nation once so strong and brave
Sent these innocents to their grave

As sleep moves in across our land
We wonder how to take a stand
To fight again for right and true
And reestablish red, white, and blue

Soldiers Did What They Were Sent to Do, cont.

Our shores and borders no longer safe
Our military lies in wait
For a true leader, commander-in-chief
Who understands our nation's needs
And once again the world we'll lead

We hang our heads as we pray
Father, deliver us this day
From shameful leaders before the world
As nations laugh with lips up curled

Wealthy politicians rule the land
Thinking We the People don't understand
The corruption and greed their power displays
God help us to be righteous and brave
And once again our country save

We need a leader with no strings
"God Bless America" he would sing
And back to our feet our nation bring
For now, we shudder in disgrace
Thirty-one August engraved on our face

First Responders and the Homeland

First Responders and the Homeland Quotes

"In the midst of the heartbreak and wreckage of 9-11, the world also witnessed what is America's greatest strength. Firefighters, nurses, police officers, first responders and local residents worked around the clock to rescue and care for those injured." ---Dan Coats

"Every problem is a chance for you to do your best." --- Duke Ellington

"All men were created equal, then a few become firemen." ---unknown

"Firefighters save hearts and homes." ---unknown

"Evil is powerless if the good are unafraid." ---Ronald Reagan

First Responders and the Homeland Poems and Musings

TERRY OVERTON

FIREFIGHTERS' PASSION

One thing cannot be denied
Firefighters are responders with intense pride
And passion for their charge, to keep us safe
No matter the hour or frantic pace

It's out the door they swiftly go
Knowing deadly smoke will blow
Inexplicable combustion and death
Unimaginably gasping for their breath

And the day you called and mournfully said
You pulled an infant from a swimming pool, dead
Your sorrow could not be contained
The resemblance of your own children strained
Your heart as it was torn, you knew
The sadness of death of those who
Loved the infant, she was theirs's
You bowed your head and said the prayers
Of one father who had seen too much
But the next day others required your touch
To pull them from a wreck or fire
Your help required for the most dire

You prayed for strength restored once more
The next alarm you raced out the door

AMERICA OF WE THE PEOPLE

Firefighters' Passion, cont.

And the time you called as you gasped,
After the structural building collapse
I knew the desperation of your task
To save whoever was in the grasp
Of the fiery torrent's path

Like all firefighters you're vigilant
You save others from danger imminent
Often thankless and without pay
You volunteer on your off days

Where would this country be
Without firefighters to whom people plea
For help when they are scared, suffering,
or pain persists
With honor and respect, firefighters assist
And aid the needy on the call
With passion and determination
You answer all

Into danger we see you turn
Into fire smoky blazes that burn
Or using jaws of death or water rescue
Whatever the charge, we count on you

Please know we appreciate your risk
As into safety you securely whisk
The innocent victims from harm's way
To Your heart dear God, we pray
Keep firefighters safe each day

TERRY OVERTON

REMEMBERING BLUE

I cannot understand
The hate brewing across our land
For those wearing the badge to protect
And now it seems we're evil wrecked
The cities are a free-for-all
No worries of crime, no one will haul
You into jail to serve your time
Take it all! Just pick your crime

Do you aspire to loot, steal, take for free?
No worries because no one will see
And if they do it doesn't matter
The cities' laws are now in tatters
Just burn it down, to be no more
Without police, evil wins the score

To those men and women who stood
For honesty, values and good
What will our country be
Without badges protecting you and me?

BORDER GUARDS

I live along the border here
And wonder if there's danger near
From gangs, cartel, and violent crimes
From those who secretly cross the line
Set by our country, now in vain
Our Border Patrol must play the game
The politicians are to blame
The border guards are sad to hear
They cannot keep our border clear

They feel helpless as they watch
The brazen acts of those who stash
Young children and women in their vans
To traffic broadly across our land

Why do politicians allow
These innocent children trafficked now?
It is not for benefit of refugee's lives
But for money and votes they contrive
To keep our borders open wide
We are no longer safe inside

TERRY OVERTON

WE SAW YOU THERE

We saw you there, ash covered face
Rushing toward the demolished place
Through fire, smoke, and threat of collapse
You went into the crumbling trap

You knew others were caught inside
Who needed rescue you provide
Through molten metal, concrete crashed
In smoke and fire the demon gnashed

You persisted, grappling up tower heights
With gear you struggled with weakening might
You swore an oath to faithfully discharge
Your duty to save all from death's march

Four-hundred twelve tried to provide
Four-hundred twelve did not survive
Firefighters, police, medical staff
Sacrificed in the terrorist's attack

Twenty years later, we mourn for you
And the families that you knew
Our hearts were broken on that day
But your memory will always stay

You're in heaven now, we pray for you
To receive the thanks and blessings you're due
Please know our hearts break every year
We weep and wish you were near

Current State of Affairs

Current State of Affairs
Quotes

"In spite of warnings, change rarely occurs until the status quo becomes more painful than change. People seem not to see that their opinion of the world is also a confession of their character." --- Ralph Waldo Emerson

"Not all change is progress." --- Woodrow Wilson

"Freedom is never more than one generation away from extinction. We didn't pass it to our children in the bloodstream. It must be fought for, protected, and handed on for them to do the same, or one day we will spend our sunset years telling our children and our children's children what it was once like in the United States where men were free." --- Ronald Reagan

"The world is a dangerous place to live; not because of the people who are evil, but because of people who don't do anything about it." --- Albert Einstein

Current State of Affairs Poems and Musings

TRUTH

Why is it so hard to find?
Truth is fact, not made-up spins and covered
up sins

The stark lack of leadership in our country
Spreads across the world
With socialism, Marxism, and lies, our freedom
now swirled
Into a miry mix of sludge
History will be the judge

Our country is watched with scrutiny
like no other
Until now, all citizens were brothers
In this year of 2021
Admiration of us is done

Laughing at our exceptional pride
Taking us down, with their hate inside
The talking heads on TV abound
Truth, where is it to be found?

REPORTING AND WRITING OF YESTERYEAR AND TODAY

---Cosell---
He minced no words,
He called them out
The truth he told on Monday night
For football, or for boxing fights
Howard Cosell was a welcome sight
Where are the Howard Cosells of sports today?
There are no truths on sports airways
Politics and knees are headlines now
"No honesty or patriotism" is their vow.

---Cronkite---
He told us when on moon we landed
When civil rights were justly demanded
When "I Have a Dream" changed to heartbreak and nightmare
Life taken too early by evil's snare
He shared with us Camelot's ending
And reminded us of hostages pending
Till their release four hundred plus days later
We need another Cronkite commentator

--- Hemingway---
To WW I reporting he did go
Ernest Hemmingway we all know
Could pen his words to touch our hearts
And reported actions of evil's depart

Reporting and Writing from Yesteryear and Today, cont.

Continued writing outstanding works
Unlike the cheap manufactured quirks
We see today in book after book
Exploding on Kindles and Nooks
Until depression won its fight
And took out Hemmingway's literary light

--- Writing today and yesteryear---

News and books have changed for worse
Cable, network, internet… a curse
Years before on news programs
It was true news, there was no spam
Or lies and spin, of trashy smut
The reporting was factual; it was just

Peter Jennings, Ted Koppel,
Dan Rather, Ed Murrow, Tom Brokaw
Carl Rowan, Bill Moyers
Marlene Sanders, David Brinkley,
Helen Thomas, And many more
Where is the honesty of years before?

BIG TECH RULES THE WORLD

Dark web, deep state, big tech conspires
Censure free speech? Facebook requires
No political posts unless you agree
To be no different than lib party

Conservative line? or religious hail?
Will find you soon in Facebook jail
Get woke or know the fatal end
Support the constitution? You're not Tech's friend

In case you think our votes are safe
From Tech's dark manipulative state
Just ask the Pillow Man, whom we all love
He'll tell you voting machines aren't above
The pressing shout of big money's lure
Not even elections now are pure

JUST BECAUSE YOU SAY IT'S SO

Just because you say it's so
Doesn't make it true, you know
You want your lie to be true
You say dishonest facts, you shrew
Saying it over and over and over
Won't make your father your mother

Just because you say it's right
Doesn't mean *Americans* were on the flight
All were vetted and found safe
Now the enemy is within our gate

Just because you say it's fair
Doesn't mean the truth you bear
All voters were citizens you say
All were living and breathing that day
The unregistered and skeletons appeared in line
To cast their forged ballots, intertwined
With those of us who have IDs
Proven living citizens, we all breathe
Demanding IDs will make you seethe
Your election results? We the People weren't pleased

We all are citizens, look at us
Unlike your falsified documents
Rolled in by suitcases and secretly stashed
Beneath the poll tables for mounds of cash

Print more! Print more! No one will know!
Just because you say it, doesn't make it so

Just Because You Say It's So, cont.

Duplicated papers of all the same mark
Cloned ballots and numbers on your chart
Your ballot chain of evidence busted
Ballot harvesting, duplicates were trusted
You secured a bogus victory
Then the basement dweller was set free

Just because you say it's so
Doesn't mean you're right, you know
And now a man in office sits
With no remorse for the offense

TERRY OVERTON

OUR BORDER FROM BOTH SIDES

Your tiny faces, teary eyes enlarged
You wait and watch for a border guard
To take you in, life secured
To escape what you do not understand
You are a trafficked victim in this land

You left with men you did not know
Your own parents could not forgo
The violent sick kidnapping atrocity
Taken to a frightening unknown city
Where criminals would soon abuse
Your trust and mind, your body used

And on the other side I see
Politicians claiming victory
They have succeeded in opening the gate
And sealed your human trafficking fate
If the politician's daughter appeared
Would they act so cavalier?

Politicians! Tell me now!
If she was your daughter, then how
A rescue would you arrange?
For these little ones, it is the same

Politicians! Are you not brave
Enough to save
The women and children trafficked here
Under our noses very near?

Our Border from Both Sides, cont.

And others who feel great charity
Want to help these little ones, but clearly
They cannot see deception, smuggling, misery
They don't know your young thoughts within
Toward those who *claim* to be your kin

The criminals know when you get in
You'll make them fortunes and they know
The cartel will be free from harm, and so
They'll get away with their crimes
You my child, free-will resigned

Unknowing Americans think it's great
To let all inside with trusting faith
They go along with politicians' plans
Uninformed Americans don't understand.

The open door reinforces
With money the cartel coerces
The crimes continue never-ending
Politicians' minds never bending
Their position, which is absurd
The cries of the trafficked go unheard

Open borders? not the cure
It won't stop dirty money's lure
The problem must be addressed
By heads of state, we demand progress
Stand strong against heinous crimes
Arrest the criminals to do their time

Our Border from Both Sides, cont.

Work with the countries south of us
Instill an international security trust
Close it down until such time as you
Know exactly who is coming through

AMERICA OF WE THE PEOPLE

IDENTITY OF WE THE PEOPLE

No matter what the media spews
It matters not your color, race, or views
We the People:
are stronger than they want us to believe
We the People:
do not hate, as media wants us to perceive
Only inept journalists feed this to the masses
We know we live on greener grasses

We the People are the majority
A majority made of everyone
It matters not the neighborhood, race,
or religion
We the People know our hearts
We will not fall for false fits and starts
We offer help to those in need
Across state lines, colors, and creeds
In hurricanes, floods, fires, or winds
You'll find us rolling up sleeves and jumping in
To help the others who share our land
We the People understand
Our anger rises when we see
Media using identity:
"Are you poor? Or brown? Or black?"
"America does not have your back"
They lie.

Ask the soldiers who serve side-by-side
No matter color, race, or creed
As they defend our nation's pride

Identity of We the People, cont.

Ask firefighters in the night
Serving side-by-side when fires blaze bright
Ask those who wear the badge of blue
They serve to protect me and you
No matter color, race, or creed
All serve to keep us safe and free

When talking heads purport myths and lies
Don't let identity categories tint your eyes
Look through clear vision and comprehend
We the People must start again
To repair the damage done
By talking heads who divide
Our country in factions, fractions, promoting lies

We are more alike than different
Pray for unity of We the People
Do not be fooled by lies

INSIDE OUT

We all have hearts that beat it's true
And eyes of green, brown, or blue
We have lungs that breathe in air
Brown, red, blond, black, our hair
Our nerves and organs are working, too
To keep us living, me and you

Our mouths can speak, sing, and chew
We are the same, me and you.
It is our minds where we depart
And in our thoughts within our hearts
Where negativity can stealthily creep
Finding positivity and love fast asleep
I choose to know and love each one
As taught by Father, Spirit, Son
I would not wish upon you harm
But smiles and kindness, love, and charm
For you to be my friend each day
I'll pray and hope you feel that way

But when you choose to believe
The media and others who deceive
You think it is your shade of color
Which makes you not my sister or brother

I pray for your mind to change
And to remember our Father saves
Us from this path of prejudice and hate
Please walk with me through friendship's gate

Inside Out, cont.

We are the same, both you and me
My prayer is that one day you'll see
Our families and neighbors are the same
And quit the evil media's game

OUR SECOND AMENDMENT

Some whose mental health is lacking
Are bitter, biased, reality cracking
Upset beyond their understanding
May grab a gun or knife in rage
Against all society to assuage
Dark demons inside their mind's cage
Masses cry "Weapons cause foul play"
But that is not what We the People say

We the People support those who suffer
We pursue our happiness alongside others
We think all Americans are our brothers
And our gun rights protect each another

So never let those in power
Who want to grab our guns and scour
Rights and free will away
We the People loudly say
Never take our guns away

TERRY OVERTON

'ISMS

Absent is true republicanism
Replaced by money, power, cronyism
No longer here, democratic individualism
It's been replaced by shouting socialism
No tried-and-true U.S. nationalism
But rather loud irrational globalism

And knocking loudly at our door
Threatening evil, shore to shore
Communism, Marxism are marching in
To steal capitalism, industrialism, from within

A new world order will divide
Us apart with hate and pride
We are to unify with them
And forget Constitutionalism

The camps soon form across the land
Racism, environmentalism, take a stand
Conventionalism, patriotism, all out the door
Totalitarianism, terrorism, you explore
And find our heroes struggle to fight
Money, evil, power behind the plight
Don't overpower our freedom fight

Stand strong, stand firm, and pray each night
To prevent an apocalyptic sight
And patriotism will shine again

'Isms, cont.

To chase the 'isms to their end
Throw the evil out our country's door
Let liberty shine forevermore

TERRY OVERTON

PANDEMIC

Mask! No Mask. Well, make it two
Government wants to protect you
A vax, no vax, oh make it two
No wait! A booster goes into you
To keep you safe and breathing well
Protecting from pandemic hell

We want the facts! The people say
"We gave them to you the first day
It was a bat, no wait a lab"
And now the mutants we all have
To fight away these pesky germs
You scrub, cleanse, no germs displayed
All social gatherings, six feet away

Now in year two we slug along
I think there is no right or wrong
Shuffling through with cautious eye
No questions, no! don't ask why
Just use your common sense I say
Until the virus goes away

GENDER IDENTITY

Male? No female you protest
Female? No, male! It is the best
Actual biology does not lie
But mine is not to examine why
Some say they're different than their birth
And wonder what their gender's worth

It makes no sense to me at all
But some desire a different call
Not as received through X or Y
Misunderstandings! they all cry

I'm male, no female, some may shout
It is a sin, say some devout
For me? I'll let God sort it out

TERRY OVERTON

Leaders Around the World

Leaders Around the World
Quotes

"Any woman who understands the problems of running a home will be nearer to understanding the problems of running a country." --- Margaret Thatcher

"The nation will find it very hard to look up to the leaders who are keeping their ears to the ground." --- Winston Churchill

"The best executive is the one who has sense enough to pick good men to do what he wants done, and self-restraint enough to keep from meddling with them while they do it." --- Theodore Roosevelt

"The greatest leader is not necessarily the one who does the greatest things. He is the one that gets the people to do the greatest things." ---Ronald Reagan

"If your actions inspire others to dream more, learn more, do more, and become more, you are a leader." ---John Quincy Adams

Leaders Around the World Poems and Musings

WHERE ARE THE CHURCHILLS?

Gruff, strong, firm, never flinching from your conviction
You led the way, amidst world tension
You fought from the losing position
And found a way, no matter the mission

Once, with the enemy firmly ahead
In Dunkirk, with strategy, you led
And rallied your country to pitch in
With boats, and ships, you did begin
To gather the boys from jaws of death
And boldly infused freedom's breath
Where are the Churchills of present day?
Where is the wisdom? gone away

With challenged resources, hope filled your eyes
You mustered reinforcements from allies
When approaching evil came too near
People hid in basements, filled with fear
You found a way to protect your shores
United Kingdom safe once more

The world has changed with malicious eruption
Now money, power, sin, corruption
Are spreading quickly hand to hand
An evil spirit permeates our land

Where are the Churchills to fight back?
Rallying the people? There is a lack

Where Are the Churchills?

How do we fight money?
How do we fight evil?
A new world order will rule the people

There is no true election present here
There is no honesty to cheer
Cheaters, liars, sinners, scammers
Where are the Churchills for today?
Honesty, wisdom, bravery, gone away

TERRY OVERTON

ONE LIFE CHANGES THE WORLD

Under the bright Mvezo sun
A village baby boy was born
Not knowing of the human hate
In his day, unjustly great

He grew and learned
Under watchful eye
And trained in leadership
Not knowing why

He wanted peaceful means to work
But in the end oppression smirked
And locked this man of peace in jail
For twenty-seven years, a cell

And Robben Island was no match
For the message he dispatched
The people in his country gathered
"Our freedom movement will not be shattered"

And when at last his freedom earned
He led the world, and we have learned
Persistent peace is the way
It would work here still today

But in our country, we must think
Of Mandela's way to peace
Our conflicts of race must evolve
Not with media, but humanitarian resolve

PEACEFUL HERO: TANKMAN

I wonder when you woke that morn
You knew you'd stand before a nation torn
Between Communism and Freedom's fight
In front of tanks you stood, no fright

A simple man with shopping bags
You waved your hands like battle flags
And said "You can't bring tanks inside
The Republic of China's square of pride
Because now, it's hosting students there
You should not be in Tiananmen's Square"

Guardian angels whisked you away
Tanks returned later that day
Then students, peasants, workers arrived
For freedom's pursuit they bravely died

PEACEFUL HERO: AUNG SAN SUU KYI

Another country fights the fight
Looking for freedom's peaceful light
A lone woman jailed, no tears
Confined inside for several years
She fought communism without fear
She bravely stared in gunmen's eyes
Who pointed weapons with shallow lies
Aung San Suu Kyi peacefully remained
Expressing boldly communism distain

To her a Noble Prize awarded
Peaceful protest: violence thwarted
Yet today conflict abides
Burmese army coup inside
Torn away the progress made
Instability now parades
Along the border China watches
Civilian, military Burmese clashes

AMERICA OF WE THE PEOPLE

One Nation Under God

One Nation Under God
Quotes

"The time has come to turn to God and reassert our trust in Him for the healing of America-our country is in need of and ready for a spiritual renewal." --- Ronald Reagan

"The reason America is a special nation is because it was founded by people who were first on their knees before they were on their feet. We are a nation rooted in our faith." --- Mike Huckabee.

"We face great challenges in this country, but we've faced great challenges before and conquered them. What carried us through was a willingness to seek power and protection from One much greater than ourselves, to turn back to Him and to trust in His mercy. Without His help, America will not go forward." ---Ronald Reagan

"History fails to record a single precedent in which nations subject to moral decay have not passed into political and economic decline. There has been either a spiritual awakening to overcome the moral lapse or a progressive deterioration leading to ultimate national disaster." ---Douglas MacArthur

"If we ever forget we're one nation under God, then we will be one nation gone under." --- Ronald Reagan

One Nation Under God Poems and Musings

TERRY OVERTON

AMERICA, WE PRAY FOR YOU

America we never knew
We would need to pray for you
In this time and unusual world
Where people think our country is gnarled
With hate and weakness on world display
Our country needs intensive prayer today

Many go about their lives
Unaware darkness soon arrives
In the form of socialism or tyranny
We the People must bend our knees
And pray God will turn their heads
And patriotism no one would dread

As if there was no need to worry
Their lives possessed by hate and hurry
Despising others; they don't understand
The value of freedom in this land

When we need strength to speak
Dear Lord provide voices to the meek
We can no longer remain silent
On God's strength alone be reliant
Together we unite in prayer
For America to have God's care

LESSONS FROM HISTORY FOR A NATION UNDER GOD UNDER GOD

We cannot look toward the future until we study the past. History tells us God allows suffering of nations when they stray away from what is right, true, and within God's commandments for us.

But does history repeat? Is this relevant today? When a nation does not follow God's guidance, will suffering come next? Can we draw parallels from the events in history to present day? One thing we do know, we can examine the events of the past and understand their meanings.

Here are a few well-known Biblical references from world history and events.

Records of people falling into sin and living lives with questionable morals are found early in Biblical history. Aside from mankind's fall in the Garden of Eden, we read accounts of sin that became a world-wide practice as noted by the story of Noah and the Great Flood during the time period of 2504 ---2404 BC.

Noah lived his life doing what the Lord asked of him. He was obedient when the majority of people of his day traveled a different path. Noah was laughed at, scorned, and in the end, he and his family survived.

Lessons from History for a Nation Under God, cont.

The story of Sodom and Gomorrah documents another time of a world gone wild. Sin, repulsive behaviors, and corruption were rampant. This was so prevalent that God destroyed the whole place. This event was around 1904 BC.

Egyptian punishments are well documented during the time of Moses. Egypt was country of kings, or Pharaohs, like those in Babylon. In these countries, the rulers required the people to worship kings and rulers as gods. Idols were not unheard of along with the worship of false prophets. Time and again we read of plagues, floods, fires, swarms of all varieties of insects and varmints. The time of Moses, between 1604-1504 BC, records these events that happened to those who disobeyed God.

The pattern repeats throughout history. Nations' values decline. Chaos happens. Crises occur. It is no surprise. It is not new.

As MacArthur noted, nations who behave with no morals do not last. Can the people of the United States look in the mirror and honestly report we are in agreement with God's principles? Commandments?

IN WHAT DIRECTION SHOULD WE GO?

If my people, who are called by my name, will humble themselves and pray and seek my face and turn from their wicked ways, then I will hear from heaven and will forgive their sin and will heal their land 2 Chronicles 7:14

When God looks down upon us now
Does he weep and wipe his brow?
In disappointment, sorrow, grief
He knows the devil is the thief

Love and values, stolen from hearts
Old and New Testaments depart
From those who once had faith in You
Tell us Lord, what to do

On my knees I cry in vain
Watching my country die in pain
Once "Under God" and in You we Trust
Replaced by money, power, lust

Is it too late?
Your faith in God, don't you recall?
Pray evil doesn't take it all
As we deteriorate, then fall
Into communistic hands
Or socialism as oligarchs plan

TERRY OVERTON

In What Direction Should We Go?

Please God awaken eyes to see
Our country is no longer free
To pray and worship as before
No cross or manger at our door

No prayer in school, no flag to fly
Dear Lord please hear us, tell us why
These evil forces cover mountains and plains?
Across the nation, Christians in pain

Can we together make a change?
Deliver us from happenings so strange
People of our nation no longer hear
The Words You breathed into their ears

NATIONS AND GOD

Blessed is the nation whose God is the Lord, the people he chose for his inheritance From heaven the Lord looks down and sees all mankind; From his dwelling place he watches all who live on earth Psalm 33:12-14

Once home of the American Dream
Heartbreaks rip our foundation's seam
No longer love of country and God within
Dear Lord help these return again

Your will be done for us it's true
It's time for us to return to You
Our prayers, faith, and love we'll bring
That You may again to us cling
And in our land return freedom's ring

TERRY OVERTON

PRAY FOR OUR FUTURE

Therefore I tell you, whatever you ask in prayer, believe that you have received it, and it will be yours Mark 11:24

It is hard to look at our world today and let go of worry
We are filled with anxiety watching the crumbling of our nation
As humans we long to control, to fix, to hurry
Until a peaceful end is found,
And our country is re-established as
One Nation Under God

Unite with others and a chain of prayer begin
To pray for God to enter the hardened hearts within
And in the minds of those who govern
Pray for our country to remain strong in
The foundation of the U.S. Constitution
Turn 'round our fate
To one with positivity and strength.
Push forward to unfathomable lengths
To bring our country back again

AND WHAT OF OUR FUTURE?

I do not think much of a man who is not wiser today than he was yesterday-Abe Lincoln

Our fathers, uncles, grandfathers, and great-grandfathers fought in the wars of recent history. One thing we have learned from them, our freedom is worth the fight.

To learn about the future, we must study the past. Remember what happened when evil infused a country or the world and apprehended freedom and faith. Is it happening today? Are the same evil forces penetrating countries around the world? Is the same evil capturing the minds of the uninformed? Will we be better tomorrow?

We must examine our country from a world perspective and know how blessed we are. Let's hold on to our blessings. Unite with other like-minded individuals. It will surely take us all to win this battle against the new culture of quick reacting uninformed non-thinkers.

WHAT ARE THE LESSONS LEARNED?

I am one person in the America of We the People. I am but one vote, if votes count anymore. We are all worried. Our nation has suffered through wars of the past, WW I, WWII, Korea, Vietnam,
9-11, Dessert Storm, Operation Enduring Freedom, Afghanistan abandonment, to name a few. We weathered a Civil War and reunited. We experienced the destruction of our economy more than once. Horrific storms, fires, pandemics, Cuban Missile Crisis, Benghazi, are scattered in our more recent history. Other troubling events include the state of lawless cities, the fate of police in our country, and the porous border.

Regardless of the losses, tragedies and victories of our history, our immediate future feels exceedingly undecided. We are looking in the faces of corruption every day when we look in the eyes of many political officials, federal officials, and government employees, media personalities, and even the officials of other countries.

Looking back, have we learned lessons? Are there signs from the past to guide our future?

Churchill was indeed a literary genius who was able to evaluate the larger picture of the world and history. He was keenly aware of the United Kingdom's place in the global political environment

What Are the Lessons Learned?

and opposing forces. He had skills not common in politicians today.

When Churchill evaluated the state of affairs of the conservative party of his day at the beginning of WWII, he was appalled by their inaction. He surmised they were simply hanging around and waiting on the locusts to come. Is the same not true today? Would Churchill draw similar conclusions to the federal administration in the United States today when looking at important domestic and world events? Would he feel the same about our conservative party?

"The government cannot make up their minds, or they cannot get the prime Minister to make up his mind…**decided only to be undecided, resolved to be irresolute, adamant for drift, solid for fluidity, all-powerful to be impotent. So, we go on …for the locusts to eat."** --- **Winston Churchill**

Where is Our Hope ?

Where is Our Hope?
Quotes

"My concern is not whether God is on my side; my greatest concern is to be on God's side, for God is always right." ---Abe Lincoln

"Freedom is the open window through which pours the sunlight of the human spirit and human dignity." --- Herbert Hoover

"America was not built on fear. America was built on courage, on imagination, and an unbeatable determination to do the job at hand." --- Harry S. Truman

"At what point then is the approach to danger to be expected? I answer. If it ever reach us it must spring up amongst us; it cannot come from abroad. If destruction be our lot we must ourselves be its author and finisher. As a free nation of freemen we must live through all time or die by suicide."---Abe Lincoln

"If you always support the correct principles then you will never get the wrong results!" ---Andrew Johnson

"My God! How little do my countrymen know of what precious blessings they are in possession of, and which no other people on earth enjoy!" --- Thomas Jefferson

Where is Our Hope? Poems and Musings

TERRY OVERTON

HOW WE BUILT AMERICA

Some of our families come from afar
From distant shores, they traveled here
Others from countries ruled by kings and queens
Or from our own land which was serene
Before a European face was seen

In centuries before our time and place
During times of primitive rough landscapes
No power or machinery there
Wild terrain countryside, completely bare

Through will of minds and strength of faith
They formed the lower forty-eight
Villages grew to cities and towns
Across the vast rivers, mountains, around
The New World was painstakingly formed

Explorers, pioneers, cowboys, preachers
Ranchers, butchers, farmers, teachers
Each person had a part to play
To establish our great USA

This does not mean the path was clean, pure or impeccable
Acts of history were intolerable and criminal
Days of old are sad lessons learned
Patriotism, respect, and honor were earned

How We Built America, cont.

> Now on the precipice of freedom's death
> You pray, "Dear God, what can we do next?"
>
> He glances down and with a smile
> He breathes the words into your ear
> "Uniting together will help you here."
>
> It is so hard to loudly say
> You support the USA
> Attacks from all sides we have found
> It's hard to start this turn around
> So many without knowledge of history
> Don't understand our freedom's mystery

Unite and take a stand to help others understand.

Freedom is precious. Let us save it.

WE MUST DO THIS

The White House is full of talking heads
Who give us nothing but moans and dreads
The inspiration is not there
For Americans anywhere

Where is a leader to stand with pride
For the feelings of our hearts inside?
There is no happiness within the voice
And masks? Vaccines? We have no choice

Now the people's office is replaced
By a teleprompter reading face
We pray freedom is established once more
And throw crooked politicians out the door

Now we hear of travel bans
For those who have no vax card scanned
On a paper for you to display
Americans in their homes will stay

I'll cast my vote next time around
And pray that honesty is found
Within technology and polling place
And we'll elect freedom's face

Let's not give up, it's not too late
As droves of voters, we should rate
The current administration practices poor
Let's vote freedom in once more.

WHAT DO WE KNOW ABOUT US?

The bombing of Pearl Harbor was a sharp wakeup call for our country. For people in our country on that day, it was the kind of alarm that shook the nation like a middle of the night panic with hearts pounding and palms sweating. It is the kind of wakeup we never think can happen; the one that sickens you each time December 7th rolls around on the calendar as we think of lives lost.

On September 11, 2001, we experienced yet another unexpected wakeup call. This was even closer to the heart of America, happening in the contiguous United States. We watched in horror as terrorists attacked our way of life.

These tragic uncalled-for events cost the lives of Americans and injured scores more.

What do we know about us? From these and other events, the great depression, surviving pandemics, and other tragedies, we know Americans are resilient. We dust the dirt off our knees and stand back up. We stand up and unite against foes.

At this writing, it is September 11, 2021. Twenty years have passed since the Twin Towers collapsed, flight 77 was brought down into the Pentagon, and flight 93 was brought down in a field by heroic Americans. It is with heartfelt sorrow we remember and honor those who died on this day along with those who died in Benghazi on September 11, 2012, and who died in Benghazi on September 11, 2012, and other terrorists attacks. And now, we can add the date of August 26, 2021, to the calendar of days when needless deaths at the hands of terrorists happened to American soldiers who were sent in harm's way.

Today, with the feeling of helplessness derived from an inactive and disappointing administrative reaction, it is challenging to pull ourselves back up from plummeting to the bottom. Our hearts remain heavy. Yet, as Americans, we know the only way to bring our country back is to bond together and lean on each other and God for strength and hope.

As hard as it may seem, this is a task which we *must* accomplish. If we do not, it may be as Churchill once said, nothing to do but wait for the locusts.

We are stronger than terrorism, socialism, and communism. We are Americans.

LAST WORD: GOD IS OUR STRENGTH

God is our refuge and strength, an ever-present help in trouble. Therefore we will not fear, though the earth give way and the mountains fall into the heart of the sea, though its waters roar and foam and the mountains quake with their surging. Psalm 46: 1-3.

ABOUT THE AUTHOR

Terry Overton is a retired university professor of educational and school psychology. She has an Ed.D. in Special Education and a Ph.D. in Psychology. Her professional experience includes teaching public school, teaching at the university level, and being a college dean. She has two children and seven grandchildren. Her writing and publication experiences include textbook and journal articles in the fields of special education and school psychology. She is a conservative Christian who is proud to be an American and longs to increase patriotism in her country. She seeks to answer God's call to share the good news and grow the church by writing Christian books and devotionals. Her book "Both Sides of the Border" is a Firebird Book Award winner in the categories of Cross-Genre, Socio-Political Fiction, and Women's Fiction. She was an International Book Award Finalist, and a Readers' Favorites Finalist. She and her husband live in the southern tip of Texas where they enjoy semi-tropical weather and spending time with their friends and family.

Connect with Terry Overton:

https://www.authorterryoverton.com

https://terryovertonbooks.com

https://www.amazon.com/Terry-Overton/e/B001ILHKPS?ref

Follow on

All Author

https://allauthor.com/author/terryoverton/

BookBub

https://www.bookbub.com/profile/terry-overton

GoodReads

https://www.goodreads.com/user/show/74738557-terry-overton

AMERICA OF WE THE PEOPLE

Other publications by Terry Overton:

Both Sides of the Border (2021) Ambassador International

Coming Soon:

The Oddball Ornaments and the Story of Christmas- (Ambassador International) A middle grade reader

The Oddball Ornaments and the Story of Forgiveness- (Ambassador International) A middle grade reader

Sabal Palms and the Southern Squall (Ambassador International)

Sabal Palms After the Storm (Ambassador International)

The Newton Chronicles: Soldiers, Crystals, and Temples (Ambassador International 2022)

The Newton Chronicles: Shepherds, Lions, and Storms (Ambassador International 2022)

The Newton Chronicles: The Narrow Gate (Ambassador International 2022)

Earlier Books published by Christian Publishing House

Devotional for Youths: Growing up in Christ

Devotional for Caregivers: Finding Strength through Faith

Devotional for those Coping with Tragedy

TERRY OVERTON

En Español

Devocional para Jovenes

Devocional Para Aquellos Que Cuidan Enfermos
Terminales, Ancianos o Discapacitados

Devocional Para Aquellos Que Hacen
Frente A La Tragedia

www.ingramcontent.com/pod-product-compliance
Lightning Source LLC
Chambersburg PA
CBHW052328220526
45472CB00001B/329